The Time of Icicles

Some of the poems in this collection have appeared in:
TickleAce
The Newfoundland Quarterly
Don't Quit Your Day-Job: a labour arts magazine
Garm Lu: A Canadian Celtic Arts Journal
Banked Fires: An Anthology of Newfoundland Poetry

The Time of Icicles

poems by

Mary Dalton

Mary Dalton (signature)

BREAKWATER

Breakwater Books
277 Duckworth Street
P.O. Box 2188
St. John's, Newfoundland
A1C 6E6

Cover: Don Wright, Sea Light, *50"x 38", red ochre,
charcoal, oil stick and pastel, 1987.*
Photo of author by Eva Musseau.

*The Publisher gratefully acknowledges the financial support of
The Canada Council which has helped make this publication
possible.*

*The Publisher acknowledges the financial contribution of the
Cultural Affairs Division of the Department of Municipal and
Provincial Affairs, Government of Newfoundland and Labrador,
which has helped make this publication possible.*

Canadian Cataloguing in Publication Data

Dalton, Mary.

    The time of icicles

    Poems.
    ISBN 0-920911-73-0

I. Title.

PS8557.A47T55 1989   C811'.54   C89-098641-X
PR9199.3.D34T55 1989

Contents

And, thou away, the very birds are mute....

William Shakespeare, Sonnet 97

...The aim must be to gain a past from which we might spring, rather than that from which we seemed to derive.

Harold Bloom, The Flight to Lucifer

the old men are dying

vanished the acrobat lovers
in their hunched shoulders
the long caress of the scythe

who will uncover
those fields reclaimed
by the dog rose
coax out again
strawberry lushness
from caplin and dung

who'll tell us now
eyes dark, in pity and scorn
my duck, sure you don't know
what work *is*

the yellow silk dress

magnolia yellow, butter
yellow of yellow roses,
sun whipped in cream
of white heifer, god-conjured,
gleaming warmer than gold, than sun,
a vinery, stitchings, thread tracings,
petals embroidered
and silk-covered buttons,
a demure line of dots,
elliptical,
gliding, *glissando*, towards
silk-scalloped waist,
slight flare of skirt
rippling to mid-calf hem

a rhapsody of curves and of silk
breathing out mothballs, faintly,
'forties romance—
essence of tangos—of twos—
hanging in the thrift store,
flirty, on the hook,
cooing, "uncrumple me—iron me,
wear me tonight,
step out in my curves,
my soft yellow silk—
i can hear the rustle
somewhere in the city
of a lean tuxedo
a dress shirt all ruffles
and golden snake cufflinks,
an emerald stud—
stars and champagne"

taxi dispatcher jazz

where you at, five five
where you headed at
pickin up a job are yah

car forty-five
Holiday Holiday
gotta go to main door—
justholdonforaminutewillyah

three six four
there by Shoppers'—
Used Cars—
there by City Motors

don't call me Harry, Darren
Roger's not my name either

St. John's staccato
barking the pockets of the city
a twitch of demented riffs
these cats under hot tar roofs
an irritable music
authentic as fiddle
            as washboard
    as any
            cigarette papers and comb

David on the Mountain

I was very far out.
The wind warned me.
On the savage peaks
I fled from Saul.
Dizzy, I saw leaping
Ibex cheat death
Along the gray cliffs,
In sky
Horns a whirling scimitar.
Chasms below, still
The Sea of Salt
Kissed the land—
Its bitter embrace.

Mocked by the salt
And the stone,
Memory whispered:
Michal,
Sheep safely pastured,
The sigh of the harp
In my hand.

Hungry,
Desert birds
Danced on Ibex's back.

how nicely they die

how nicely they die
fainting among ferns and lilies
those man-made
pre-raphaelite lovelies

how those painters and writers
relish their white fading
mewing in the tranced
death-laden dew

yet flame flickers in those waters;
some ironic Muse begets
on these teary necrophiliacs others:
women of fire, their children of fear

wild cassandra wanders
on the edge of those drowning verses
A fire dances before her, and a sound
Rings ever in her ears of armed men.

empire's other flag

In London in 1847 the work-house paupers were given the job of crushing horses' bones. They were so hungry they fought one another for the gristle.

a sulphur sky
two scarecrows tussle
one's down
a rasp rises up from mud
and heaps of bone

"listen mate
these bones are mine
tackle them horses over there
you can see my mallet's
been having a go here
half the work of crushing's done
your red little eyes
are drooling for this gristle
take your spit somewhere
these bones are *my* dinner"

the wind gusts, swirling
soot in billows—
a dark cloak
over horses and paupers—
motes from Newgate
the black dome of St. Paul's
Smithfield's
blood and foam

their rags flap—
Goyaesque—
empire's other flag

if i were water

if i were water
i'd lap softly round you
you'd swim in my waving
i'd coil you
to dolphin
you'd frolic in seas

The Journal

It's March the ninth—
no feast of any immaculate conception—
and winter in Newfoundland
for supper Joseph Drouhin's Fleurie 1985
one bottle grands vins de bourgogne
and—appellation contrôlée—
one hour of *The Journal*
and—Barbara Frum,
after the passion
the true passion
ungainly absurd
of the child care issue
I recall best
the whiteness
and width
and the breadth
of your gleaming teeth
as they flash
before question
after answer
your lips' timing
exquisite
as a dance of iambs

Teeth are power
teeth and your judicious smile
and your pale apricot—
or is it peach—suit—
with the cream silk (white linen?) blouse—
I feel your passion
more painful even
as you orchestrate
more painful

than those women who strip
for your cameras
some strangling in their mothers'
pearl chokers
some twirling uneasily
a circle attached to a cross
trying in their nakedness
to tell how it is
make it better
make it right
make the best
of all possible worlds
epics of pain
tucked into platitudes
their voices crying
(yielding to fathers
their monumental absence)
I'm a mother grandmother
lawyer who nurtured her child
her baby   hen   infant   her blue   her milk

civil civilian
you orchestrate
their passions
yours the illusion of control
your controlled response
is a pain—a grimace
beyond their earnestness
your synthetic sincerity
a wound
beyond their pain—
an honour?
your coat of arms shines
you are so well-bred

still.   your pain
has a limited imagination
your journal and your silk blouse
can't find a way
to let speak
my mother my sister
with the dropped uterus
the ugly dress
varicose veins and no options

Horsey

When the horse whinnied over
And said let's swing baby
She thought—not very long—
Haven't heard of horse AIDS yet—
He's got a strawberry coat—
Lean shanks—
A glossy rump—
And that rolling eye!
Bet he can canter
With the best of them.

Honey she said
You're the best offer
I've had in a long time—
And those wings!—
'Slong as you don't ask me to
Sleep on straw
Wear blinkers
Eat oats or design feed bags
Watch *National Velvet*
Breed centaurs
Boycott Ascot—
Well darlin'
I'm good for a gallop—
A roll in green meadows—
Or a long trot under the stars

like moving massive stone
to write those days:
out behind the house
our father poised on his gray rock throne
broken leg stretched out before
arms enshrining his fiddle

such content
in his content—
rare content—
held in the dance
the banshee twists
the fiddle and the sun and
the rooster's racket
in that almost-cacophony
the only true quiet
in our house

our father speaking
fluent
shackles fallen
moving in his world
of tune

A Scythian Boy Loses his Faith

The air is a red mist.
My eyes blur.

We carry the head
through the long grass—
blood paints green
blades red
splashing from a red ring
knife-poem
cross-section:
muscle, blood-channel, bone.

The stave lies,
narrows to sharp point
to hoist it
to blue mystery
over the chimney's
slow column of smoke.

Its eyes are fixed
forever, on us, for us.
Safe-keeper, old men say.

I cannot believe.
From those grey balls
an endless eddy of hate.

Interview

for my student F.G.

Together we pore over
the tangle of phrases
chaos of words half-
understood half-hitched
to others misspelt floating
commaless no thought train
we are both lost in this cave

he looks up from the webbed paper
shakes his head as
if shaking off flies—
a burst of himself—
words free from the page—
—y'know
i sweated bugjuice
over that!

Song for Dandelion

Because it mirrors the sun.
Because it cheers waste spaces.
Because it ignores orders.
Because it is a wanderer.
Because it sings in this acid soil.
Because its roots are coffee.
Because its flowers are wine.
Because its seeds are a circle of mist.
Because it puns.
Because it has lions' teeth.
Because it is invincible.

chapel's cove ghosts

fleeing the april city
we enter our pasts together
together climbing in the wind's teeth
to stoical cliffs looking east

weather has eaten the lone house there—
gray, it crumbles to dust
through glassless windows
it welcomes the wind

we move carefully in the ruins
you venture the stairs while I
stand among remnants of stove—
brown ribbons of wallpaper curl

signs of a lost grace everywhere
in splintered fragments of moulding
detailed as some old slow dance
white porcelain door-knob, a wallpaper rose

your steps sound softly overhead
down the wind's avenues you
glimpse your years past in this cove
your californian dream of roots here

foregone now, the garden and the stream
the land sloping down to beaches and the
distant harbour—a heritage house
in the city and a new woman

below, beside the crazed stove,
funnel, warming oven askew, rusting
legs of nickel holding up the body intact
I am a weary palimpsest

in the sheltered cove behind, my mother's past—
but I had climbed these hills, inched
down red rock cove below, only to play—
this fading house abandoned even then

at sixteen I clutched the future in my hand
for my mother's dreams my father drove me to the city
(some peninsular dream of sun and ease?)
college nuns chopped at roots, all jagged edges

now, bone-chilled, each alone
we wander the corpse of this old house
seeking what? some sign
that we were here? that somewhere
in these frail timbers lurks
a record or a prayer?

wind-battered
we huddle our way to the car
your brandy flask warms us both
as we head back to the city

Polyphemus with his eye out

Remember, Doris,
such men are dangerous—

sobbing between curses, he
blunders about the shore
ranting of his lost power
admitting his essential
folly—
his girth barely
smaller than his ego—
and bellowing
his monumental love

hungry, hungry, he
begs you to bandage
that raw and bleeding gap
pledge an end to time's tide
call up mussels for supper
and sing him endless
lullabies of sea

thanksgiving day

thanksgiving day
holiday
on gower street
the jackhammers play—
are the men shaken
in the jackhammers' grip
grateful—
arc-ed, conjugal
enfolding the juddering drill
those shudders eating their hearts

the thrift store

at the threshold
he pauses,
tentative, quavering,
frail torso tilting—
but still a lean old hound

"i'm lookin' for a pair of shoes—
have ye got a pair of shoes today?"
the girl fishes out a battered brown pair,
cracked, seamed, but soles and uppers intact—
"just these, they're not very good—
not your size—
maybe on Monday—
sure you're in here every day—
see what we got on Monday—"

nodding OK, he wanders about,
fingers the racks of last decade's fashions,
yesterday's furniture,
the chipped, stained, faded, outmoded, outgrown,
the virtuous cast-offs of the ever-acquiring,
the upwardly-mobile

now he's poised to tackle the steps,
three, down to the glass door
and out to Prescott's buzz

the girl watches, sunny, benign,
calls after him
mentions the weather—
"what you needs is a little garden"

over his shoulder
accepting her gift
he gives in return
the riches of ages
in his throaty reply,
his gravel amusement:

"i'll be getting a little garden soon
yes i'll be having a little garden soon enough now"

quick as *he* is,
the girl comes back,
at once meeting, avoiding:
"oh you won't be getting
that kind of little garden
for a long while yet"

all sequins and silver
Sweetn's and Bowring's
don't carry this fashion

dressed in wry humour,
taking Death's measure, mocking
his rawboned solemnity,
he repeats
his green recognition:
"yes i'll be getting a little garden soon"

retrospective from under the waves

snip
the scissors cut
the cord
first separation

seemingly

lines already severed:
grandmother
grandfather of both houses
for history a silence
white house with red trim
brook stable out-house
white circles on the ochre
a gilt oval photograph
sepia colour of history
a bearded man
with hard watchful eyes

again the blades flash
ending connection
with father
with mother
before the bonds grown firm
grew clear

in the silence
a fiddle
and a green dress
with black roses

removed to the museum
of others', adult memories

wary of ties now
tied that knot
the Gordian knot
snip
the scissors cut
he's grown invisible
before my eyes

blade-keepers,
holy women,
no more.

i float adrift,
i plummet

i like to turn around that corner
find the foxglove in your garden
its spotted sheafs of coral bells
a silent peal of *gaudeamus*

Larry's Nightmare

or; living with contradictions

The creative-writing professor tells his shining class about making
    the big time
Chalk arc-ing in air he intones addresses, contacts—
The room lights up, neon flashing 6-foot letters: BOOKS CANADA
It's just possible to earn a living as a writer in Toronto, he confides.
If you want to be professional, you've got to go where the bucks are.
In mid-spate he pauses, uneasy: unbidden, filling the room,
    knocking over the *Toronto Publishers' Directory*
Three long-haired harpies hissing mocking, three Newfoundland
    harpies ripe
Transforming into Sheela-na-gigs, screeching at him through
A haze of Jockey Club, of Labatt's Blue: poetry is of place, poetry
Is of presence, you are a huge absence, you wear the colour of void
You dream television commercials and your touch is the kiss
    of deodorant.
Their keening voices spin, draw him into a vortex, but
The university professor, calling upon the spirits of CBC
Of Canada Council of Hockey Night in Canada, pulls
Himself together out of that bag of tricks, reaches for the nearest
Globe and Mail, rolls it into a wand, a cross, a publishing contract
With McClelland and Mulroney: the harpies shiver,
Shrink, their voices dwindle to leaves to ashes to smoke.
Shaken, his words strange in his ears as a script he hasn't quite
    learned
The creative-writing professor continues the session: now, as I was
    saying...

diminuendo

a lone bee tumbles towards
ragged petunias, their torn
veined skirts a memory
of name worn like a banner:
Summer Madness

the bee nears the rosy tatters,
veers, falls in slow ellipses
away to nowhere,
its tired gyration
tracing the end of summer

Mexico 3

Near dusk we sit in the *Zocalo*
in white stone love-seat, companionable S
two among the evening crowd.

Then a boy, eight years or so,
tired black eyes and
shoe-shine box on back
stands before us:
Pesos! Pesos!
A demand.
No.
Si! Pesos!
No.

He stares at the man, not me.
Si. Muchas pesos, gr-r-ringo!
He rolls the word. Sliding liquid from his tongue
It becomes beautiful.
Another beauty
lies in the balance:
his rich contempt merged with his yearning
for the glory of pesos
lying unattainable
in *gringo* pockets.

the song of the talking heads

the cafeteria is dull pink,
dull grey—
some decorator's dream.

around the circle tables
we talk about the weather
fog frost a summer burn-up perhaps
the options are fog or smoke
we talk of downtown destruction
maybe next the Hall will go
a towering monster in its place
we talk about the Constitution
will they   won't they   why should they
slowly sandwiches are consumed
styrofoam cups decorated and crumpled
the gaudy pie vanishes
fork after plastic fork
occasionally glances cross
sentences collide

in the nightmare cross-hatchings
of the pink-and-grey Henry Moore
couple embracing
faintly
Virginia Woolf is whispering down,
a rustle of autumn leaves,
"under the conference tables
bodies?
or long thin stalks
on which the heads
come to rest?"

eyes touching eyes—
—a laugh ricochets—
topics in shards,
notes scatter in
the song of the talking heads

The Community Field Worker's Invisibility Reel

Once I was down in Burin
Carting around the big old cameras
All the equipment we used to have—
Picked up a fella I knew in high school—
He said gone into television repairs are you now Dan

Another time in Millertown
A woman came running over the road
She wanted a quart of milk—
Thought I was the milkman

And one time in Parkers Cove—
In an old red van that time—
They thought we were the CN Telephone—
Wanted to know
When we were putting in the 'phones.

It's hard sometimes
Tellin' people
What you do do.

A Litany

for Judy Chicago and Don Wright

Crimson joy
      Enchant us
Mystical rose
      Appear to us
Temple of pleasure
      Bless us
Torch flower
      Bloom for us
Wave furrow
      Caress us
Throne of delight
      Receive us
Eye of eros
      Behold us
Amaryllis
      Tremble for us
Petals unfolding
      Enfold us
Jade gate
      Open to us
Dawn's brightness
      Glimmer for us
Blood rose
      Pulse for us

Evaluation Rag

Dracula dripping carbon
From pedantic jaws
I pause
Draw another needle-sharp
Valor 131-B
Eagle Canada
From a host in squat stone pot
And proceed to pierce the heart
Of one more tender essay

Meanwhile
Along the hall
Emile's fiddle
Its fierce sweet wail
Mocking these leaden manoeuvres

backhome blues

we walked and were unwelcome
on road where asphalt met encroaching alder
no path for walkers here

several chickens in every pot
and cars poised in landscaped driveways

our relation to the land's
grown problematic
a nibbling absence hovers
over these toy bungalows, these neat drives

this road's not chapel's cove road
a path to jimmy hawco's house
to sue's big meadow in back
to the church over the ridge—
they walked over like goats in winter

this road has never heard of the cliffs and the sea
it barely notices the ponds alongside
this is a road to somewhere else
dallas las vegas los alamos

car-culture.   cars ferry
the children of walkers
somewhere else.

there's one barn
on the mile of road we walk
its curving roof alien
as the pre-fab bungalow beside
a fairy-tale barn

if we climb the long driveway
lift the massive latch
we'll find within smurf
cut-out sheep, goats, chickens
yellows and dusty blues

so many houses are fenceless
the smurf animals never stray
into nextdoor's smurf-patch
of calendulas, orange ghosts
of cabbage-rows
lettuce, beetroot, the carrots
of winter

still the land remembers
the night releases its old smells
wild roses water and grasses

street lights cast a fluorescent
sheen on the ripples
the moon has been cancelled

the overgrown meadows make a gift of their smells
a slow fist is squeezing my heart
as we walk through our land conquered

and no-one fired a shot

the acrobat act of wresting
a living from reluctant
earth, quaint tale of old times here.
here is a toy-town, vision
of mr. disney and mr. ford

resettlement of the mind

Lies for the Tourists

That rug was hooked by a sweet white-haired grandmother
For love not money.
That fish is fresh, caught by that strapping young feller
With not a care to worry him—he loves the sea.
That harbour the sun gleams bright on is so-true-blue—
No poison here.
Those children playing in the crooked streets—so friendly
So quaint—
Are fed on the milk and honey of our simple island kindness.
Those starlings strayed in from the mainland,
Their mad cries an alien sound on our shores.

Transylvanian

It's the yen for that Dracula love,
The cape, the black cravat,
Those opium eyes, the voice like honey,
The flaring of those aristocratic
Nostrils—

Oh for those deliciously pointed
Snowy teeth to sink
Into flesh, needle in, suck out
Will, life-blood, dull day.

Take me, we cry, unbuttoning
A million lacy negligees—
Here's flesh, silky, look,
Here's blood, more than
I know what to do with.

We swoon, murmur,
As he bends, saxophone, over us,
Of course, of course,
I'll follow you anywhere.

porno 2

he makes love like a battering ram
as if he's got to build a road
blast his way through the high passes
and come out fightin' those pesky redskins

he makes love like a battering ram
as if he's in a race with Rocky IV
pumping steel thrusting with his might
into the insatiable maw of the universe

did someone tell him there was
something terrible up there?
needing drumming into submission
with offerings of blood and sweat

she has become a cairn   a pit
the wounded earth
the ruthless derricks
drilling deeper deeper

Mrs. Gamberg Has Chopped Down the Tree

Now I lament the dead maple
And the bitter O of its stump.
Because its leaves sang in the wind.
Because it caught the sun in its branches.
Because it caught the moon in its branches.
Because it sheltered the black-and-white cat.
Because Emma climbed it one day.
Because its leaves sang in the wind.
Because it budded in spring.
Because it made rust and gold in the fall.
Because it raised its head in the sky.
Because its black lines remembered summer.
Because it stood over my garden.
Because its leaves sang in the wind.
Because its shadows played on my house-walls.
Because a green spirit lived within.
Because it netted electronic music of starlings.
Because it cast a green spell on Flavin.
Because the very old woman next door
        had loved it.
Because the man who planted it
        had loved it.
Because it lived through glitter storms.
Because it stood fifty winters.
Because it sheltered my small garden.
Because its shadows dappled my garden.
Because its leaves sang in the wind.

St. John's Day 1987

St. John's Day is now a Week.

At the Village Mall a Village Coke Castle.
One million cans of Coke
With a disc jockey inside.
Toothsome treats—
Buy Coke for the Janeway.

Cod-tongue-eating contests.
(*Tongues of fun for everyone.*)
Fish nuggets (Horton's Locker)
From Fishery Products International.

Fish and Chips Competition
At Bowring's Captain's Cabin

Molson's offers a Beer Waiters' Race.
Buy Molson's Gold—
For the Big Brothers, Big Sisters Association
Of course.

The Canadian Paraplegic Association
Is organizing
A Mock Jail—
Head of the Pond, Quidi Vidi Lake.

Step-dancing
Courtesy of
The Downtown Development Corporation.

At the Northwest Atlantic Fisheries Centre—
Fascinating tours.
And film showings—every two hours—
Ten Days, Forty-eight Hours,
Depicting the lives of offshore
Fishermen and their families.

Behind the Murray Premises
Hangashore Dory Races.
At the Curling Club
Kaos and Dog Meat BBQ.

he calls me his Hecate

1
he calls me his Hecate
i think of drowning his storms
in the seas of my hair

does he think of the Titan's daughter
blessing, ruling over
horses, wars, farms

or furtive creature of night
haunting cross-roads
queen of ghosts and magic
hell-hounds her familiars

or Artemis' sister
old mother moon and midwife
the earth cradled between her legs

i stand in triple form
looking down the three roads—
at the intersection, turning to stone

2
he calls me his Hecate
no magic, no malice
just a tag he heard somewhere
the language wags him, little dog

3
he calls me his Hecate
i shiver—yes—with pleasure
his words are kisses
he kisses me all over

our spells outface Mr. Death

4
he calls me his Hecate
i accept the frame
all smiles and silence
i keep to myself
his names, his frames:
Procrustes, Tantalus
and that fellow
chained to a rock
his liver picked out by birds

Forlorn gentlemen—
right this way

King Lear
come speak to me
let me comfort you
for Cordelia's loss.

Is there a Hamlet
          in the room?
I'll take him on—
devotee of the futile
seeker-out of
the hopeless cases,
the ones whose mothers,
trying, loved them.

I am,
if not your Sargasso Sea,
your Conception Harbour
your Trinity Bay.
Wherever I am
there's room for three
You, your ego, and me.

Even semioticians eat

after Philip Stevick

The word is
a signifier
this flesh is
signified

something is
missing
lost in
(in)elegant *formulae*

the curve
of my hand
round this pen

in the beginning
was the word
the word was
made flesh

this word is
a small round stone
kidney
or opal

under the sign
boulangerie
this bread
this word
this wine

Regatta Villanelle

As summer speeds towards our regatta,
It flaunts its fleeting prime in flower and tree:
Sweet pea and candytuft exult in green cantata.

Sly runner beans plot riot in loud poinsettia,
Each trellis rife with talk of leaping free,
As summer speeds towards our regatta.

Mallow leads honeysuckle in soft sonata;
Meadows, lanes, and lawns sing harmony.
Sweet pea and candytuft exult in green cantata.

Now winter's tribe forgets its fierce vendetta,
Its knifing winds remote in memory
As summer speeds towards our regatta.

Bee-kissed, the purple monk's-hood sways, far from biretta;
Pistil, stamen, anthers writhe thick with ecstasy;
Sweet pea and candytuft exult in green cantata.

Now 'round Quidi Vidi's blue they swarm, all social strata,
Afire for races, or masses—or for some weighty fee,
As summer speeds towards our regatta.
Sweet pea and candytuft exult in green cantata.

Enos Watts at the Breakwater Launching

Everything about you
fluttery, light:
the beige shirt
high light voice
from your rippling face

meeting my praise
deprecatory murmur
hand's gentle clasp
light brush of kiss
on my cheek

you begin
gentilesse
share-words for golda—
golden wife—
for lisa and jade

quiverings
"if you will"
"as you know"
thin filaments
spun for the crowd

now: from the light web
arises, *clarus*
that dark heavy music
strong, savage, wise
as the night-laden cliffs
as the heart of the raven
black turbulence
with the perfect gravity
of stone

What sort of woman would you fancy, Nelson?

What sort of woman would you fancy, Nelson?
'Cause I've more than half a mind I'd
Fancy being the sort of woman
You fancied, Nelson.

You wear riverboat neckties—
Would you fancy a bustle, honey?

Your raw bay consonants thrill me—
'Though you grew up in Gander, Nelson.
I speak good bay my own self honey—
Perhaps not the Notre Dame kind.
Still—

What sort of woman would you fancy, Nelson?
'Cause I've more than half a mind I'd
Fancy being the sort of woman
You fancied, Nelson.

'Cause you're a demon-angel on those keys, Nelson,
A gentleman-caller of my very own kind—
And your throaty beaked call, honey—
What sort of woman would you fancy?

The 'Forties

My Dad didn't look like Humphrey Bogart—
Something at once sharper and softer—
A young Dick Tracy perhaps,
Handsome like a blade and a puppy.

My Dad didn't look like Humphrey Bogart,
But my Mom looked like Ingrid Bergman:
That refined voluptuousness,
That silky voice, those cheekbones, a waist
Curving in from amplitudes.

They were seventeen,
Born in one parish—
Separate coves, worn paths between.
The 'forties had swept them away

To Argentia, silver city,
The streets paved with Americans.
They wore badges with faces on them.
He moved large objects
From one place to another.
She wore a frilly apron
And waited on tables.

She learned restaurant *mores*.
A crane dropped on him
One smashing block of concrete.

After, they lived across from a lake,
White house by a stream,
Mid-way between two coves
In one parish.

Her table settings were immaculate.
His knee no longer bent.
She tied his shoelaces.
In church, surrounded by genuflection,
He slouched,
Not sitting or kneeling.

Evenings were rosaries, she led
The Sorrowful Mysteries.

now is the time of icicles
now, Nootka, I cast off
my summer name
hold hard my winter name:

I am become Wolf
anew
dancing grinning among clowns
drumming
a song so vast it
pulls your world down

garden codes

Those scarlet runner beans
      just sprawl everywhere. Later,
the scarlet blossoms give way
      to beans green and sweet.

These are bleeding hearts
      broken in the last storm.
The fleshy stems are so fragile—
      they snap in the wind.

And these are morning glories:
      they bloom—blue—for a day.
Blue trumpets with sunshine
      at the heart.

leo lapierre on cbc

fast—
on the heels of our fat fears
of sikh refugees
mine-sweepers in the persian gulf
dollars . . . so many billions
transactions not completed—
the sly, wry strings
plucking the rhythms of water
plucking quick ripples of dance
and the gravelly voice of leo lapierre—
stone lion of my heart—
unfolding his story of music made
his music made
from oatmeal boxes
sardine tins
an old spitoon
and his wooden puppets tapdancing away
to his tunes

his English elegant, its accent
wearing a lilting French shadow
he tells a nation of sikh-fearers,
silk-wearers: my strange instruments
. . . to make something
of something nobody wants . . .
. . . to be happy with
the place where you live

exquisite simplicity
too small or too large
for our ears

the words fade into lute-like
strings the puppets dance
the news moves on
leo lapierre's lost
in some vast tinnitus of our soul

logos

chapter five: one fat chapter:
cancer of the reproductive organs
abstract words crochet a comfort:
dysplasia cryotherapy
prognosis positive or otherwise
the names proclaim themselves
territory conquered by naming
allies of neat margins
elegant type sane drawings

cosy conspirators, they cluck,
everything is under control
feminist doctors wrote this book

everything is under control
no colour photographs
this is not a medical text
written for young men in Porsches
no black sores
on this mystical rose
nothing of that thin yellow
odour of death

delf and the children's games

his notebook and his listening ear
make a door, ajar:
along its slant of light
slopes away
green gravel, green gravel
your grass is so green
grandmother gray
london's bridges, falling down
ringing 'round rosies
all falling down

statues
giant's steps
here we go
paddling in the ducks' water

go in and out the window
    in and out the window
go in and out the window
as we have done before

red, blue jackets flapping,
calls shrilling down the years,
the children careen
into the ducks' water
away from grandmother
gray, the falling bridges

time's dark horizons,
all misting and blurring,
turned arches, exultant,
in their cathedral of play

storms

"He could make a puddle of her, with his fierce desire."
—Alice Munro, *"The Beggar Maid"*

first soft scatter of snowdust
moist paperweight spirals
polite snowkiss on cheek
intimations a caress
pleasures of anticipation
drift down
languorous blowing on Garbarek's sax

eddies come faster swirling
wavelets of white over windows
now sky's an icedove
hovers over snow-world
muting the spasms, the
spinning discords as the storm
hots up

howling his hunger
the North Wind arrives
in a passion of ice
wolves sing in his red eyes
fires of the steppes
whirl now in his arms
turning turning
he shows basilisk
the gleaming eye
of the berg

For Rainer Werner Fassbinder

The announcer's voice is crisp, competent—
One more item in the Arts News items:
"German director Rainer Fassbinder
Was found dead at his home.
Aged 36 Fassbinder was
One of the most prolific
And arguably the best
Of Germany's New Wave of directors.
Murder has been ruled out."

Media-gray, the bland prose oozes;
You shrug, unsurprised—
You were, after all, a most keen connoisseur
Of evil's faint mediocre.
You knew that fear eats the soul;
You wept the bitter tears
Of Maria Braun, of Petra von Kant,
You who moved among wolf-children.

You painted
A nation gnawing at its own vitals
The colours of defeat

And tiny islands of love
In the tired greens of apartment houses
The sneers of the neighbours
The old woman and her black *gastarbeiter*
Snatching joy from the jaws of the dragon.

Now you move beyond argument,
Alert among your images,
The tawdry obituary a clip
From some movie you didn't quite finish.

she counters auden and others

The poet is the father who begets the poem which language bears.
W.H. Auden, Poets at Work

the trouble with your stuff
he said, smoking,
is that you don't take men
seriously enough

i gape—i'm amazed
they're everywhere
stars of my show:
talkers, lovers
fathers, workers
villains, listeners—
stern women
have warned me
of my unhealthy
obsession

what can he mean?
(a mean-blues mean?)
perhaps he glimpses
his irrelevance in my verses
line-maker himself
knows the lust of the form
to play with(in) itself

language murmuring to itself
its own lullabies
pacts treacheries swansongs
spinning labyrinth games

or does he sense danger:
my turning from him—
my briarless joy,
all girdles off in wily
word-spangled play?

perhaps it goes deeper?
he fears an unthinkable cuckoldry
his earth-wife
mating with his word-wife,
language, begetting on her
bastard children who know
no father

i smile,
knowing the rat in the arras,
use no dagger,
embrace him
assure him
that i take men
very seriously indeed
and invite him
to come up
and see me sometime

april wind

the wind is insane tonight:
against the house it sweeps
sheets of rain, hissing
an idiot's persistence,
the skirt-swirling
of a fawning woman,
mouth slack, lunatic
with love, her susurrations
monotonous, interminable,
soft insistences of chiffon
inexorable as sea

gauzy, foam-dancing wind,
salty Salome,
not-quite-right Aphrodite,
sidling up to mind
now's needed
a north-easter
        to cut like a knife

dawn song

there never were larks—
first light sent crows
hurtling down over plum trees
strangling in the cork-death's grip

caw! their black whoops
ricochet 'cross the hill
void made flesh
maddened accordion, wry carnival

there never were larks—
those mornings brought clamour—
fierce, Bedlam-glad

crows
composed the day
in pearl-eyes

up behind the house
the wind tumbling
a ragged black feather
over the mound of ashes
potato peelings
and dish water

the crows knew:
once, unbidden,
potato shoots had risen there

my lover is a forty-six-year-old virgin

my lover is a forty-six-year-old virgin
he writhes on an executive-grey *chaise longue* all day
he longs to be swept away

Tantalus of our time
(O the golden grapes the sparkle)
control is his disease: he's dying of it
Spartan coin, he's the other side
of Little Nell, Beth, *La dame aux camélias*
he hears them taunting him from the century's grave

women light vigil lights for his pain
perhaps he'll become an insect or a breast
know ecstasies of the passive verb

he's dying of power
he caught it in the street once
the New Lie in its well-cut suit

women light vigil lights for his pain
pray for the grace of his seduction
into realms of velvet and flowers

you've noticed how stray cats get that way—
the wary turning of the head, the
low growling over a surprise gift of fish,
the quick hiss and retreat at the proffered pat

you put it down to accumulations of
kicks   brooms   boots, being chivvied
from yard to yard, sidewalk to fence to tree
legacies of ships' cats and Christian tradition
(plus—it must be said—a bit of pissing in the dahlias)

still, knowing the symptoms is no defense
as you watch yourself growing forty and difficult
snapping at gentlemen callers
cringing, suspicious, ready for the boot

paterfamilias 3

weekdays, with his shattered knee
he stood on concrete floors
listing, doling out bits of machines
for McNamara's, then for Golden Eagle
(cousin to the warbirds at Argentia
money for limbs money for limbs they cry)

evenings, he sawed wood, chopped splits,
mowed hay, swung coal in buckets
filled hoppers for chickens
slung feed to penned sheep and goats

Saturdays, in the family store
he hefted sacks of sugar and flour,
sliced bologna, cheese, plunged nicked hands in brine
(answering the plea, "give me a nice piece now!")
retrieving the fat-marbled hunks of beef—
he filled the Hillman with cartons bursting
with groceries for Gallows Cove

later, the hairpin turns and Furey's Tavern
navigated—she just wants to pull in there,
he said of the Hillman—he set
potatoes, carrots, cabbage to fill
sacks waiting in cellars mouths waiting in winter

nights he stretched on the curved kitchen bench
soon asleep beneath the newspaper
face hidden, below the headlines and the ads

now at last moving in his cage of days
i see him one Saturday standing at the scales
taunting his Smallwood-sponsored university nephew
with his failure to master the *Weekend* word-puzzle
his own mind like lightning among numbers and
words

one of the baffled ones
bones picked by merchants and warbirds
shaking his bars at his simple nephew
looking across twenty years
at a world with time to read and play

Medusa and Dracula

Beneath a gibbous moon, beside a boiling sea

Medusa and Dracula set out for a walk.
He averts his eyes;
She looks out for her neck.
"So much *Sturm-und-Drang*," she scoffs,
"All this blood-renewal, eternal life,
That messy striving of the undead—
My lovers are luckier;
One brave glance gains them
The elegant serenity of stone.

But then—"
As snakes writhe in the pewter light—
"Women, labyrinthine, wrought in you,
Incarnate, their necessary image of love."

paterfamilias

some kind of lethal quicksilver
you elude my grasp while burning
brands deep in memory's flesh

scars overlap, merge, layered pains,
sedimentary accusations, lies, commandments
savage with the certainty of centuries

now, as your bones melt in the graveyard,
to name you, write out your composition,
tugs at me, icy imperative of science and love

let me count the ways i fail to know you—
bone-counting, scene-listing, tales
of storms outfoxed, gashes sewn, timber chopped

now so much shifting ash, you hide
your wily, wiry self among
clichés of stillborn fictions

Aoife

sea-bird
he turned you—
bad wife
alphabet-thief

thought to jail you
the sky your cage

you twisted in blue
already planning
the bag's design—
the secret letters
beating in your blood

the bag made
of your own skin,
you slowly reclaimed,
your skull

the white horses
whinny
as you soar
    you soar
    overhead

Almost

I brought you sage seedlings and a magazine
We walked in your garden—I
Admired the violas
We spoke of plans
For future gardens, not mentioning
Each inner drought,
Seed of these fine blossoms

I walked home later, the poem
For you
Still folded in my purse.

old houses' secrets

old houses yield up secrets
in coves not far from here

the urine smell
of old ones'
dying within

mouse mold-damp,
a house's tears:
why have you left me
no flame

the kitchen listening
a salt shaker turning
to clotted salt and rust

bedrooms a rectangular
gape—
stands drawerless,
awry—
the fungi rejoice—
no baskets embroidered,
no china birds, shepherdesses

in his frame
Leo, Pope
of unlucky number,
offers to bless—
his verdigris fingers
his plaster and gilt
loom over
an empty stair

carpenter cows
on slow pilgrimage
on fields of painted canvas

blank
giving nothing away
windows stare down the lane
the neighbours' TV
flickers back
los angeles grey

onto the ocean
the roses
the old house's secrets

kitchen

open the porch door.
when you enter
her smile and the blast
from the woodstove
heat you—to the marrow

she brings the flowered plate
the Christmas cake
the gold-rimmed
glass of sherry

seal, pigeon,
buxom galleon
she slides her bulk
behind the table

"—twenty-five widows in this cove—
we get together and play cards"

she's had two offers,
one from the cabbage man
he knocked one day
took out a wad of money
asked her if she'd marry him

the other she didn't know at all—
he came to the door,
asked if she had cows to sell,
then—just like that—
she laughs, crinkles
at her remembered surprise—
asked if she'd marry him

she shuffles the deck—
in the stove with a thud
a junk collapses into
the inferno beneath—
the air ripples, in waves of heat

spring

rhubarb's rosy tumescence
green spears of the chives
bleeding hearts'
pink and cream tips
pushing up through
earth still in love with ice

the thyme shrub, stroked,
springs back pungent
light-hazed hills of Greece

the eroding nymph
pitted by wind and snow
a shadow of her old self—
in her lap a dust of snow—
lifts again
one thin arm to the sky

the hens are gone wild

the hens are gone wild
they're ploughing the gardens
meeting in circles
of scratched dusty ochre
under the glossy-leaved tree

they drop eggs
in the hayloft
up on the hill
abandoned in grasses

a plump-chested whir
they flap up into air—
a flurry past fences

the night roost's
a mutter, a huddle,
shapes faint in shadow,
heads curled under wings,
busy,
brooding on flight

their wattles quiver
as they bend to the hopper
their small eyes
are black points of light